All Scripture references taken from the KJV of the Bible, unless otherwise indicated.

Freshwater Press, USA

ISBN# 978-1-893555-73-0

Paperback Version

Seasons of Grief, *Prayer Book and Journal*

Table of Contents

Seasons
of
Grief

Freshwater

Freshwater Press, USA

Holidays

Is it time for the holidays again? Time seems to fly after you get to a certain age. Unless, as they say, if you're not having *fun*, then time just drags on.

Holidays aren't always a happy time. Things happen on or around holidays and at family visits that people wish had never happened. It can be a very stressful time for many.

After seasonal solstices (depending on which hemisphere you live in), the days get shorter, and the sun shines less. The lack of sunshine affects a lot of people negatively, and they get the wintertime blues. There's a lull in their spirit over these darker months. There are a lot of things affecting people seasonally and all year, for that matter. Folks with the wintertime blues can be no fun to be around but our hearts of compassion go out to them.

Sunshine is needed to produce Vitamin D, and sunlight does other good things for the human body, including helping your state of mind. Something physiologically in their body is the cause to why blue people are blue, so we try to understand.

However, we should ask if there is a spiritual component to all this wintertime blues talk, because some people are blue year-round. Doctors know a lot, but God knows so much more. So, we should look deeper, spiritually.

Spiritually, cyclical, seasonal grief could be *programmed grief.* What does that mean? It means that grief has been programmed in your **family's calendar**, altar, sent to you by an evil wisher, or as the result of an evil ancestral covenant. You may start moving forward, finding happiness once more, but then another event, occasion, or anniversary comes up – time to be blue again.

Your family may embrace the tradition of the other shoe dropping all the time--, more sadness, loss, mourning or grief. Real, immediate, necessary grief, or rehearsed, age-old grief—your family may endure both individually, or together as a family. It's expected. It's what you all do. It's what happens in your family. It's the way it's always been.

You may believe that all this grieving either individually or collectively as a family or group is *love*. You believe that's how you respect the dead--, by being blue and sad.

It's not.

Exercise:

Am I blue? Chronically blue?

Am I healthy? So, if I'm sad, is it grief, or am I lacking nutrients in my system?

Prayer for Healing and Good Health

Father, in the Name of Jesus, You are Jehovah Rapha, the LORD, my Healer. I know that I am fearfully and wonderfully made. You know how everything about me works. I ask you for divine healing in every system of my body so that I can be healed, make me whole and able to serve You and my family in the best way possible.

Give me Wisdom to make wise dietary and exercise choices for optimum health. Thank You, Lord for hearing and answering my prayers, in the Name of Jesus, Amen.

The social media way of handling losses is to wish happy birthday on the Earth birthdate of the deceased, acknowledging that they are in Heaven. Since the dead know nothing (Ecclesiastes 9:5), I'm sure this is for the living.)

Man that is born of a woman is of few days

and full of trouble (Job 14:1).

Google says that celebrating birthdays is a pagan tradition. A bunch of religions don't allow it. However, we are not talking just about births, there are people who celebrate the date of a person's *death* by going into grief and mourning all over again at that same time every year. It's like having the wake and funeral every year. That's the way to stay in and increase the grief in your life. Too much grief and prolonged grief in anyone's life can be dangerous, damaging, and devastating.

While it is dishonoring to forget the deceased; it is a curse to have one's name cut off from the Earth, to be forgotten and remembered no more. But the deceased cannot be promoted in death to celebrity status. Balance must be had in all things; we should let our moderation show, (Philippians 4:4).

In the case of a lost parent or spouse, I know people who begin their mourning and grief at least a week out from the deceased person's birthday, date of death, wedding anniversary date, Mother's or Father's Day,

Christmas, Thanksgiving, Resurrection Sunday, their own birthday, the birthdates of their own children, Memorial Day, Veteran's Day if the person served in the Military, Fourth of July <u>and</u> Labor Day, if here is a memory of summer family cookouts. Add to that, any special days they shared that are not known holidays, such as first date, engagement date and other sentimental occasions. By my count – if that's about a week leading up to the date, sometimes two weeks ahead and a week *after-* - I've counted at least 20 or more *weeks* of intermittent, *planned* grief during a year with 52 weeks. This does not include any new and unexpected grief.

Planned grief and constant memorials, unless God told you to establish a memorial to Him, is not honoring God, or your deceased loved one.

Exercise:

How many days a year do you estimate that you feel grief?

Do you think of God as much as you think of your lost loved one?

Do you honor God as much as you honor your lost loved one?

Anything/anyone put before God or above God is idolatry. What do you need to change to be sure you're are not moving into idolatry?

Prayer Against Idolatry

Lord, I know that idolaters will not inherit the Kingdom of God. I do not want to miss Heaven or aggrieve You in any way. Lord, I repent, in the Name of Jesus for any thing, or person I have put ahead of You. I repent for spending more time, thought, energy, resources or love on anything or anyone, living or dead, than on You. Lord, forgive me and wash me clean and renew a right spirit in me, in the Name of Jesus. Amen.

Tidings of Comfort & Joy

And the angel said unto them, Fear not: for, behold, I bring you good tidings of great joy, which shall be to all people. Luke 2:10

And the Angel of the Lord declared, *"Tidings of Comfort and great Joy."* Comfort and Joy is not just for Christmas it is for the entire year, all year.

In Isaiah, prophetically these tidings were sent to the world before Jesus ever got here, long before His ministry ever officially started. Man was living in a world where there was no comfort or joy, so God sent Jesus to save us. At that time, there was only the Law: follow these rules or die. But there is no comfort in the Law. There is no joy in the Law.

Jesus came to give us Grace. There is comfort in Grace, and there is joy in Grace.

Life can be hard, even devastating sometimes. Perhaps you need Comfort and Joy in your life, in your house, in your world.

This book is not just about Christmas, unless it's about Jesus being born into your heart and into your life.

This book is about the New Year. Every year, all year. It is about New Year's Eve that you spent with a loved one who is either gone completely from the Earth or gone from your life. It is about the New Year's Eve that you *didn't* get to spend with the someone that you dearly wanted to spend it with. It is about the New Year's Eve party that you went to with that special someone but that was the last time you two were together as a couple, or at all.

Friend, all these things have happened to me; you are not alone.

This book is about that next day, New Year's Day when there was disappointment and perhaps you felt that there was nothing to look forward to.

This book is about the days and weeks following where the sun did or didn't shine, but it seemed not to shine in your world. The anticipation in your heart had ebbed or reached a solstice making it seem that the sun was not sufficient to shine on you.

This book is about the Valentine's Day or days that you spent alone or disappointed that you didn't get a date, or an engagement ring. It is about the *grief* of those times.

It is about no springtime surprises, no chocolate bunnies in decorated baskets. It is about missed birthdays, or birthdays where that special someone was no longer with you, or even with the entire family.

This book is about the anniversary of that day that keeps happening, repeating on the calendar that just has X's on it. Which day? Either the happiest day of your life up till now, or the saddest day in your memory. It is about that missed or best anniversary, ever.

It is about the birthday that no one remembered. Or it is about the birthday that you always treasured and you're afraid that people will forget someone that was so important to you, even if they passed on 40 years ago, so you keep posting it and reposting it online, and in your heart and in your mind.

In your soul.

This book is about the turkey dinner that's not the same. The pecan pie that is store bought instead of homemade this time because no one knows how to make it, *like Grandma*. It is about not even wanting to put up the holiday lights and wreaths, because, *what's the use?*

But it's the holidays all over again.

This book is about the tears that you cannot un-cry. It is about the heart that was either long broken or recently broken that you don't think can heal or un-hurt. It is about the heaviness that you carry around that may feel like it weighs as much or more than the weight of the person or the thing, the opportunity, the family, the career, education, house--, whatever you lost that opened the door wide enough for Grief to walk into your life.

This book is about Grief.

It is about Grief that walks into your house and takes a seat. And you expect it and talk to it.

You are not alone.

I see you.

Mostly though, God sees you. I only see you through the eyes of God. I love you and I am here to offer you tidings of comfort. Also, and eventually Joy. Yes, believe it--, *Joy*.

And although Jesus has come and done His good works and has been resurrected and risen to the right hand of the One that sent Him, some of us find ourselves in a world that still needs comfort, and it still needs joy. Sometimes that world is our *house* when we get home from a busy day.

Sometimes it's our house *all* day because we are not busy.

We all need the Comforter.

God is Merciful; He is so good.

The Spirit of the Lord GOD *is* upon me;
because the LORD hath anointed me to
preach good tidings unto the meek; he hath
sent me to bind up the brokenhearted, to
proclaim liberty to the captives, and the
opening of the prison to *them that are* bound
Isaiah 61:1

Jesus is the one that will touch, bind, and mend hearts. The Word of healing is for us, but we still find people in a season that should be joyful, when we are supposed to be blessing the coming of our Savior and representing Him to those who don't know Him, yet.

But even some Christians are heavy. They are not having Joy. Sometimes, even believers find themselves still stuck in the same vortex that the people who are living in darkness are in—needing comfort and joy.

Prayer for Salvation in Jesus Christ

L ord God, I believe that Jesus is the Son of God the only begotten of the Father. I believe and confess that Jesus came to Earth and died on the Cross. On the third day, God resurrected Him. I believe in my heart and confess with my mouth that Jesus is Lord and I invite Him into my heart and my life today and I am saved.

Thank You, Father,

Amen.

Accepted Salvation: Date:

_____

Baptized Date:

_____

Holy Spirit Filled Date:

_____

We Need the Comforter

Jesus wept. So can we. No reason why we shouldn't.

Perhaps your loss wasn't very recent. Perhaps it was this time of year and the memory of it is back. Even if it wasn't this time of year, maybe it's the first Christmas without, momma, or daddy or grandma… Or the first season without your special person. It might even be a child. It's the first birthday, Father's Day, Mother's Day without your loved one.

You are flooded with memories. We all want to be able to separate good memories from the bad ones. We want to separate the ones that lift us up and make us smile from the ones that bring us down-- but we are human and sometimes we can't do that. We may start out remembering a funny joke or something they said, or a pleasant time we shared, but it may degenerate into a sad moment or a time of the blues.

We need the Comforter.

You could feel a strong disappointment that seems like such a hurdle to get over at any time if you are grief-stricken. But Jesus, said, *Let not your heart be troubled*. He's saying He has come to do a different work in you to help you out in your *soul*.

If your soul is not strong enough to bear the onslaught of emotions and feelings, grief can afflict your soul. Grief comes to oppress you, to press you down, to weigh you down, to make you stagnant and remain in one place. You have to rise over those things that are trying to distract you, oppress you, or worse. How you do that is uniquely you. Prayer, time in the presence of God, hobbies, perhaps time spent with good friends who can inspire you.

There is an appropriate time for grieving. In the Old Testament it was 30 days in the case of Moses, (Deut 34:8). Of course, those people were GOING **somewhere**—they were going *through* the Wilderness to get to their Promised Land, so they couldn't come to a standstill because of over-grieving.

Are you also **going somewhere** in your life? Career? Family life, or have you already *arrived* and have nowhere else to go, and nothing else to do? If you are still living, moving, and having your *being*, you are needed. You are needed somewhere, by someone, for something. And let that thing be of God. Amen.

In the Old Testament when Abram's father, Terah lost a son, Terah stayed in the same place, Ur and grieved. **Grief** wouldn't let him leave. It wasn't until Terah died that Abram left Ur, at God's instruction and Abram's name was changed to Abraham and Abraham became great.

Jesus said, *Let the dead bury their dead*. (James 4:14). The Word says man's life is but a vapor. We may think life is dragging on when we are not having *fun*, but it really goes so fast. So, shouldn't we keep it moving, on to the next moment, the next pinnacle the next destination point in the Lord? Again, Amen.

There are points, places, times, seasons, and people all through *your life* where God has commanded a blessing for you. You've got to keep progressing and moving forward. You've got to be in the right places at the right times and connected to the right people.

Grief wants to defeat you and one way of doing that is making you stop and stand in one place for the rest of your life.

Prayer to Receive the Holy Spirit

Father, God I invite and receive the Holy Spirit in my life today. The Bible says that the Holy Spirit prays for me when I cannot pray for myself, when I'm going through the struggles of life, In discouragement, frustration, oppressed or at a loss for words, When I don't even know what to say. When I'm down, when I'm lost, or feeling overcome, I need You LORD.

I invite and receive Your Spirit, Your Holy Spirit now, in the Name of Jesus.

Help me see where I've failed, & where I fail- -& lead me to the changes I need to make in my life. O Holy Spirit, pray with me, pray for me. Be my intercessor today, now, in the Name of Jesus, as I bring my needs and requests to the Father. I believe I receive, in the Name of Jesus. Thank You, Lord, Amen.

Am I stagnant, or am I progressing in my life?

Grief Traps

God tells us in the Bible not to worry in that it becomes a sin for us. The things that God tells us not to do are things that let the devil into our lives. Worry. Fear. Doubt. Sin. Lying. Cheating. Unforgiveness. Bitterness. Works of the flesh.

Let's say a person does go into worry, fear, or stress, for example, this opens a spiritual door that should remain shut. Clinging on to and rehearsing old memories that make you unhappy, playing the blues, singing the blues are all grief traps. Any songs of unbelief (in God) and pain, suffering, losses, (tractors, trucks, girlfriends, boyfriends, dogs) all lead to a backward life. Backward dreams, backward progress, means that destiny cannot be reached.

(Please note the spelling of the word, re-HEARSE.)

Do not re-live the pain of things that don't improve, enhance or bring goodness and *life* to you.

Prayer Against Backwardness, Stagnancy

Lord, I come today to ask for the Fire of the Holy Spirit to burn off everything in my life that is promoting backwardness, reversal and failure in the Name of Jesus. Everything, including grief, anger, laziness, procrastination that is in my life, I bind it and cast it out in the Name of Jesus. Lord, reveal to me how I can move forward in life. Open doors for me and give me Your divine favor, in the Name of Jesus.

Amen.

Soul Tied

If you move into grief or stay there too long, the *spirit of heaviness* will come upon you and that opens the door for depression which is a pit that is very hard to get out of.

A tied soul is not a good thing or a God thing. Being soul tied doesn't mean that you're a romantic or that you loved that person more than anyone or better than anyone else ever did or could. **It really means you don't know how to love.**

I'm not judging; I've been soul-tied before.

Being soul-tied means your soul is fragmented. Either because of *codependence* – a problem you have, and/or it means that your soul, or part of it has been *captured* by the enemy of your soul--, the devil. You are not supposed to be trading your soul for anything. Not anything. If you are willing to lose your mind, will or intellect to get, have, or be in a relationship (for example), you are fragmenting your own soul.

It's not always you – sudden terror (trauma) can also fragment your soul.

A fragmented soul is easier for the devil to capture. Divide and conquer is a real thing. Your WHOLE soul is something to be reckoned with, but if you're willing to chip it away *yourself*, by being soul tied or lingering in prolonged grief, the devil can grab it or parts of it and put it on sale in the basement of… hell. Without a whole soul you are becoming weaker in the spiritual things of God.

That's the plight of a fragmented soul.

Grief is a trauma. The devil loves trauma– emotional or physical; he uses it to get you to open the door of your life to him. Sometimes in the form of Grief, but he shows up in other forms, too. The *spirit of grief* is from the devil, not from God. God is love, not grief. God is loving caring, merciful, compassionate. He understands grief, and we have a mandate to move on with life.

We are created in God's image and likeness, right? Let's see how God handled His grief in the Bible. Yes, God has had, and has grief. God through Jesus who is touched with the feelings of our infirmities understands our feelings. That's why you can talk to God about how you feel; He understands.

Truth: Every time we sin, it grieves God.

And it repented God that He had made man, (Genesis 6:6).

God has suffered losses. You may say that God didn't lose anything. Oh, He didn't? Jesus, His only begotten Son.

One of the cruelest memes I've seen online is that God got Jesus back so it's like He didn't lose anything. Let me say that losing Jesus, even for those three days was a terrible loss. Further, God lost ALL of mankind until Jesus came to win us back. If you are one of the people who doesn't understand that, then you are one of the lost that God is still grieving over. God desires that not one (human) be lost.

Jesus grieved over the hardness of men's hearts, (Mark 3:5). In Luke 19 Jesus grieved that Jerusalem had missed the day of Her visitation.

And we can grieve the Holy Spirit (Ephesians 4:30). Negative talk, rage, uncontrolled emotions, lying, stealing, drunkenness grieves the Holy Spirit, even today.

How to get past grief: Accept your emotions. Process them. Pray. Spend time in the presence of God.

God re-establishes some things when mankind grieves Him. So, SET SOME ORDER in your life. Set NEW order because that's what God does when He is aggrieved.

JESUS wept, forgave and went on about His Father's business.

Holy Spirit is kind and merciful and gives you another chance, and another, and another, until the end of chances. Then God may remove His guardian angel from you, turn such a person over to a reprobate mind. At that point, a guardian demon strolls into your life if you just want to keep sinning and not repent. I'm saying that even God sometimes will just walk away from something that is <u>repeatedly</u> aggrieving Him. These are Biblical examples that are for our edification and use. Amen.

Grieve for a season. Express your grief to God. When friends come to comfort, receive their comfort, if it is of good counsel and with compassion and wisdom. If they are like Job's friends, pick the bones out of the fish they are serving, first.

Be in grief, for a season, but

DON'T LET GRIEF GET IN YOU.

You're in grief and may feel like you can't go any lower, but from here – *there is lower.*

As many as have not this doctrine, and which have not known the depths of Satan, as they

speak; I will put upon you none other
burden.
Revelations 2:24

There **must** be a transition, an upturn
from the downward spiral of grief, or a person
can go lower and lower.

There Is Lower

Long term grief comes in bringing worry and depression. The door to your mind and heart is not just open, it is not just propped open, it's as though the door is REMOVED (not by God), so there is no spiritual protection for you right now.

You may be pining away, wishing, yearning to have your loved one back. Let's say it's a former boyfriend, girlfriend, husband, wife you have now begun the process of *conjuring*. The world may call it manifesting. **If what you are trying to get is not of God, from God, and permitted by God, it is witchcraft**.

Don't close this book. Pay attention.

If the person you want so badly will not come back, and you can't accept it, you are soul-tied. You have soul-tied yourself to them or the relationship. Now, this may not all be your fault, but it may all be your problem. Guys who are "playing the field" string women along, giving just enough hope to hang on-- breadcrumbing them since they know the women really like them, so the women remain hopeful and available. These "waiting women" may or may not begin to date anyone else believing that one day Mr. Dude will be back.

It's like the fairy tales we were forced to feed on in our childhood-- White horse. Handsome prince. Happily, ever after.

Mr. Dude ain't got none of that.

This is devil work on the part of that man, and I will now tell you why... and *how*. While you are pining away for Mr. Dude (Ms. Dudette), or your lost loved one, the devil sends in a wringer who we will call, Mr. Magic (or Ms. Magic).

One day (night) you see your "beloved" in your dream life. You can't wait to report to another friend who knows little to nothing about dreams, *"Oh, I saw him in a dream, we were together again."*

Later, another dream. *Oh, we were having a picnic together*. Another dream –, every night or so--, another dream. The dream "relationship" progresses. Next you all get married in the dream; you're so excited because this **<u>proves</u>** to you that he misses you too, and he really loves you.

It proves nothing, because it's not Mr. Dude in your *dreams*. When you want something so bad that is not of God, you form a soul tie. **The devil is in every soul tie, not God.**

Next dream--you are getting physical and having relations and it seems so real. Because it is. This seems like a very nice solution to loneliness and perhaps physical needs that you may desperately believe you have. You can't wait for bed at night. You'd rather be alone than with friends right now. What a juicy secret, you may think, and the sex may be mind-blowing.

Yes, I'm keeping it real. 100.

Reminder: the Bible says to bring the body under. That means your personal, physical body--this is what fasting is for, for example. So, these *needs*, desires and lusts don't take over – even in the dream state. Keep reading…

So, these emotional and physical *needs* make you go home after work and have a nice bubble bath, a couple of glasses of wine or maybe a sleeping pill-- all to help you sleep. Maybe you own a *personal relaxation device* (or two) – you know to "help you sleep" and you justify that with, *"Well, it's **my** body."* Studies say that millions of women do this to "help them sleep." The world's report says it's OK. **God says it's not**. Whose report will you believe?

There you are sound asleep. What went on last night while you were sleeping?

You have no idea.

It is never a good idea to have no idea of what is going on around you, even while you are asleep. The way you know what is going on around you at night is you are *dreaming*. And you get **correct interpretations** of your dreams.

Next thing you know you may be seeing shadows in your house. Hearing noises in the night. Feeling the bed go down as with a weight on it, but no other human is there in the bed with you. You can't move or speak; this is sleep paralysis. This is **spirit spouse**. You may have conjured him up with your powerful mind, your desperate needs, in your chronic **grief.**

Spirit spouse doesn't just happen because of grief, there are other ways they show up in people's lives, but this is a common and dangerous path as it relates to pining away over a lost relationship, no matter how that relationship was lost.

You don't believe me? *Where did those scratches and marks on your body come from?*

Thank God that Jesus sent the Comforter.

There is Still Lower

Oh, there's lower from here. Satan has depths. How low can he go? All the way to the Abyss in eternity, but for now, we must know his tactics.

If the person you are pining away over is deceased and you are remembering, recalling, daydreaming, pining away, wishing, fantasizing --- you can't bring that person back. You are actually conjuring up **hell** into your life. The night events may begin just as discussed with a live person who broke up with; someone who jilted you, perhaps. **Dream sex is real.** It is sex in the dream, in the night, with some entity *masquerading* as someone that you will accept. It is **not** that person you want it to be because they can't come back to you. Do you really think God will break EVERY rule and let a deceased person come back to, of all things, have **sex** with you? It's not even a person, it's an evil *spirit*, a demon.

Women have complained about being attacked in the night for CENTURIES. I know it to be true. The sleep paralysis, the weight on the bed, the "sex dreams" --I know it all to be true. This thing is called *spirit spouse* because it makes a covenant with you that you may or may not even know about. The dream marriage was a trick marriage – *it* married you. Now that it has, *spirit spouse* does not want to leave; it believes it *owns* you.

It goes lower than this, soon your dreams are **gone,** and you really don't know WHAT happened last night. You might know you had a nightmare, or a night terror, or you keep having the same dream over and over, but you don't know what that dream is. Dreams are your view into the spirit, but some dream-manipulator *spirits* can cause you not to know what you dreamed, or what you did in your dream. Ma'am, Miss, Sir: they are doing whatever they want to you, especially if you are having sex in the dream or **eating** in the dream.

Getting rid of this thing is not a five-minute prayer. Some have worked for **years** to be rid of spirit spouse. Also, there are more than *30 types* of spirit spouse. If you don't get rid of spirit spouse, it goes into your generations. Yup, right down your bloodline. It is not gender specific, it will attack your daughters *and* sons.

Perpetual or resident Grief may have opened the door; perhaps that is where yours really came from. This **thing** could have been having sex with everyone in your bloodline for generations. Yup. All of you.

My point? Grief, deep grief, depression, in my opinion are places in **hell**. You are in captivity in the spirit, although your body is here on Earth. No part of you or your soul needs to be in hell. I'm telling you, do not go there willingly. **Yearning** for the dead is not of God. This invites the devil into your life. Even if you say it was God that you were praying to, when you are asking something unscriptural, ungodly—God's not hearing that prayer. The devil may answer.

Depends on how persistent you are, how long this pining away has been going on, the next person you meet in **real** life, not because you're desperate, even if you are, or feel you are--, but because there are **no doors or spiritual protection on your life**. You're doing what you want the way you want but God's no longer in it. You may be a person who is angry with God because of a severe, sudden or devastating loss.

Warning: Don't let your prayer life go down!

Prayer life? Worship? Going to church? Are you even appreciating God in any way at all?

Has your spirit bittered to the point of, What is there to be thankful to God for?

If you are not prayed up, the devil can send Mr. Pretending to be Mr. Right into your **real** life. This new guy may look and smell good. He may be perfect for as long as it takes to earn your trust, get the keys to your house, car and life. Then he will show his true colors.

What does this mean? I don't know. But you will.

The devil likes to traumatize, torment, steal, kill and destroy. A weapon sent against you in the form of a relationship may be whatever hurts you the most.

This is a conjured up physical spirit spouse, even though it's a **real person**. (It's one of the more than 30 *types* of spirit spouse.) He is on assignment; the evil spirit in him is older than dirt. A typical report you may give or hear from a friend going through this is, *"There's nothing out here; the men these days are just horrible.,* while *wondering why* she's attracting these types.

Spirit spouse. Obsessive. Jealous. Controlling, spirit spouse.

No, I'm not trying to add veracity to the line, *'She was asking for it,"* that the ignorant or criminals throw at women, but be sure you have your spiritual walls of protection up and that you are **not asking for anything from the devil**, not even while casually complaining to your friends. We can have what we say.

Prayer to Break Soul Ties

Lord, in ignorance or rebellion I have tied myself and my soul in an ungodly way to _____. Please put your Sword between me and _____. I renounce and repent for the sin that caused the ungodly covenant, soul tie, whether adultery, fornication or other ungodly sin which I ungodly committed. Please Lord, forgive me and remove the iniquity from me for having committed this transgression against You, and also having sinned against my own body.

Lord, cleanse me from all unrighteousness; make me pure again so that I am not defiled. Lord, heal my heart, and renew a right spirit in me. I ask and believe I receive, in the Name of Jesus.

Amen.

Prayer & Deliverance Against Spirit Spouse

Start here to be rid of spirit spouse. Fast & pray, but you may need to go for Deliverance.

Father, in the Name of Jesus I come today to serve a decree of divorce from every spirit spouse that believes it has married me, in the spirit. No matter where spirit spouse came from, I declare and decree that I am married to Jesus Christ and I have no agreement, contract, covenant, marriage with spirit spouse whatsoever.

I renounce and denounce spirit spouse and demand that they must leave my life, my house, my marriage, my family – anything or place that has anything to do with me. I burn, destroy and return all items in my possession in me, or on me from spirit spouse, I do not want anything of yours, especially symbols of marriage or weddings.

Spirit children, I denounce and renounce you. Lord, send our mighty angels to retrieve and separate any of my DNA from any synthetic, evil or other types of offspring in the Name of Jesus. I decree that today that I am free from spirit spouse forever. You have no rights and no need to return to me forever. Forget my name and lose my coordinates and location, in the mighty Name of Jesus.

Amen.

Prayer for Spiritual Protection

Lord, let me dwell in the shelter of the Most High and rest in the shadow of the Almighty. Lord you are my refuge and fortress; my God. In You I trust. Save me, Lord from the fowler's snare, from deadly pestilence. Cover me under Your wings. In

You, I will not fear the arrows or plagues of the day or stalkers in the darkness. Do not let me fall, Father. Let no harm overtake me, let no disaster come near me or my home. Send angels to guard me and keep me in all my ways. Let them hold me up so I don't even hurt my foot on a stone.

Thank You, Lord, I have power to tread on the lion and the cobra, the great lion and the serpent.

Thank You, Lord, that You love me, and rescue me, and protect me and that you are with me in any trouble.

Thank You for the blessing of long life and satisfaction, Your Salvation, and that I may see many good days.

In the Name of Jesus, Amen.

Fear Has Torment

Oh, that can't happen to me. Really? And as long as you are holding on to hurt, grief disappointment, bitterness, unforgiveness--, mad at GOD or any other human, for that matter--, even it you are living in fear – all of these things could come upon you. And they all have TORMENT. There is no door on your life to protect you from these things, even **torment**.

A tormenter can be spiritual, as in your nightmares and night terrors, sleep paralysis and worse. A tormenter can be also a real, physical person, influenced by a spirit to torment you. It could be the person you are dating. Lord, Jesus – please don't marry them.

A tormentor could be your own family member, your own children. We all love our children, but that grown, adult, abusive-to-you-only tormenting child that won't move out – could they are on assignment to torment you? Don't hate your kid; spirit spouse hates your natural children and may be tormenting *them*. So, when creating or conjuring up a spirit spouse, you are bringing **torment** onto yourself, your current children and down your bloodline into your ***generations*** unless you do something about it.

Now you know.

Hey, don't do anything to your kid – **YOU** REPENT. You seek deliverance for the stuff that's in your heart, your body, your world, and watch God remedy the whole situation. It may not be instant, but God can do it!

Your tormentor could be your boss at work—next thing you know you want to quit your job. Perfect! Spirit spouse wants you broke, busted, disgusted and poor, so no one else will want you, and it can control your life. These are jealous, evil, dangerous demonic spirits.

Sins have torment. Unforgiveness and bitterness both are sins, and both have torment. Someone or something will torment you until you repent, get deliverance and resist the devil.

Dissatisfaction

If you are chronically dissatisfied, you are a perfect match for a lot of different evil spirits. Spirit spouse comes to mind because it is never satisfied. The grave is never satisfied. Lust is never satisfied. Pride of the eyes, pride of life –, never satisfied.

The "*horse leech*", understands sin, whose daughters are fornication, envy, and idolatry, which are greedy like the leech and *never satisfied. See Proverbs 30:14-16.*

Instead, if you resist the devil by exhibiting the Fruits of the Spirit, you draw more of the same to yourself to the positive.

Depression is a long-term heaviness, an oppression. Talk to God be honest, you don't have to act like you're happy if you're not. Say how you feel, how you are hurting, but look for and seek *the upward turn,* (Philippians 3:13). Something inside of you should be **thanking God** for the opportunity to have met the person that you cherish, that you have now lost and terribly miss.

Are you thankful to God to have been with them, in their company?

Are you thankful for the times you shared with that person, the life you shared? Aren't you happy about the life's experiences, purpose, and destiny you shared with them?

My mother, who has transitioned from Earth, was the exact right mother for me; *Thank You, Lord.* My mother's mother died when she was five. I thank God I was not 5 when my mother passed. Thank You, Lord. But my mother didn't **BELONG** to me; she **belongs** to God. She was my mother on Earth for the season that God indicated, but her spirit, soul and body belong to God. He says when she should stay, go, or be. My mother breathed, lived and had her being in Him; not in me.

Draw that line between sadness and deep grief, try to reach a balance. Then move forward looking for an upward turn with thanksgiving. ***Thank You LORD for what You gave me, even though I don't have it anymore***, *I'll take what was imparted to me to propel me forward instead of being regretful and mournful of what I don't have.*

I was soul tied to a guy for years, until I prayed to break it. The Lord revealed to me that part of the issue was I liked *myself* better during that time; it wasn't all about the guy. I was soul tied to the **time period!**

It seems that people are not satisfied because they are not thankful. The entitled ingrate never gets satisfied, and never says, *Thank you* to others. They especially never say, *Thank You* to God.

When you start counting your blessings, your blessings will start counting themselves. The Holy Spirit will joyfully join you and remind you of the goodness of the Lord and all that God has done for you. Amen.

Dissatisfaction is always saying or thinking *"I want more, I want different, I want what I used to have,"* instead of learning to be content is **not** the hallmark of a prospered soul. The Hebrews came out of Egypt and wandered in the Wilderness because they were discontent and dissatisfied; both are wilderness attitudes. They didn't prosper in their souls, so none of those who came out of Egypt went into the Promised Land.

You must sever ties with discontentment and dissatisfaction. My brother says, *You'd better get glad.* That's scriptural: The Lord has made me glad.

For thou, LORD, hast made me glad through thy work: I will triumph in the works of thy hands.

Psalm 92:4

Idolatry

If you are never satisfied you never say, *Thank you.* Not to anyone. Not even to God. If you think that God took your person, that God didn't do it right, you are in idolatry in more ways than one. The first way is you are worshipping the deceased or departed. Further, that person is made into an idol and your perpetual grief is the *worship.* Your mind is on <u>your</u> lost loved one all the time, isn't it?

I've seen people just randomly go to their cell phones and queue up a picture of their dearly departed several times a day, in one case their person has been gone *10 years.* They believe the person is "still with them." The dead know nothing; they are not *here* with you; that is a guardian demon, familiar spirit, or a spirit spouse. *Guardian demon* is another type of spirit spouse.

Years ago, I worked for a widower. At the end of each workday, he'd go into his office, take out an 8x10 framed photo of his first wife from his desk drawer, pour himself a drink and just look at the picture, pining away. Rumor was that this man was horrible to his first wife; that he was abusive to her in every way. Now that she's gone (20 years), he's exalted her to a new status. (Oh, he had a new wife of about 10 years at that time.)

Yes, grief is real. Grief that's *in* you brings on more grief and full-blown grief is assigned to delay, stagnate, ruin, steal, kill opportunities, destroy your other relationships and lives. **Grief wants to drag you down to death** where your dearly beloved is.

Do not agree with Grief!

I've seen shrines set up in homes where a person never had one picture of their relative before, but now that they are passed on, there's a whole shrine-, and in the living room! It's why the angel argued with the devil over Moses' body, so the people wouldn't set up a shrine and worship Moses (Jude 9).

Sometimes God will take an **idol** from you for your own good. Your not being able to get over a lost *idol* is proof that it was an idol, and that God was right. Again.

In the Book of Genesis when Jacob, Leah, Rachel, two handmaidens and all the grandkids finally left Laban, after 14 years, Rachel stole her father, Laban's idols. Laban came running after them, not to get his daughters or grandchildren back, but to get his *idols*.

When God takes an **idol** from you, it's for your own good.

Secondly, you do not know more than God. None of us do

Prayer Against Dissatisfaction

Lord, in the Name of Jesus I ask you to take away the *spirit of dissatisfaction*, the *spirit of entitlement*, and all ingratitude, pride and arrogance. I am sorry for being so unappreciative and I accept the work of Jesus and the Holy Spirit in my life to make me a better person by developing the Fruit of the Spirit.

You said in Your Word that You will satisfy me with long life. You said in Your Word that Your presence will satisfy me. As you make me glad, make me satisfied I will give thanks with a grateful heart, and I will praise You cheerfully in the Name of Jesus. Amen.

Count Your Blessings. Name them one by one.

Work to Do & You Have Help

Wherever the person is that you have lost, you don't want to go where they are. You have things to do **here**, still. Their season of being where you are has passed. Thank God for the intersection of your lives.

Further, your relationship won't be the same in Glory.

If you are saved and have the Holy Spirit, He will help you. Holy Spirit is the Paraclete, the Helper. But a person can't HELP you until you ***begin*** the process.

Now it's time to get up out of that pit and place of heaviness. Commit to press forward; the Holy Spirit will help you. Take some steps, brush your teeth, brush your hair take a shower, put on some nice clothes, and

get out of the house… then there's the Holy
Spirit right there with you.

Prayer to Invite the Comforter

Blessed *be* God, even the Father of our
Lord Jesus Christ, the Father of mercies,
and the God of all comfort;
Thank You, Jesus for releasing your Spirit in
the Earth and sending us the Comforter. Holy
Spirit, thank You for being in my life. I need
you today as the Comforter. Let the
Comforter, *which is* the Holy Ghost, whom the
Father has sent, abide with me and teach me all
things, bring all things to my remembrance and
comfort me as I go through life and especially
these challenges.

In the Name of Jesus, I pray.

Amen

Flesh Comforts

When upset, man usually seeks his own brand of comfort, most often it's comfort for the flesh. When many feel heavy, sad, sorry, they may reach for flesh comfort such as drugs, alcohol and other sins. **Even satisfied flesh cannot satisfy what's missing in the soul.** Dissatisfaction is a *spirit*; you will never successfully oppose a spirit without using **spiritual weapons**.

This discontentment is a form of idolatry and blasphemy where you are accusing God verbally or non-verbally that God didn't know what *He* was doing when God took or allowed So-and-So to be taken from your life.

Even if you are not a whole soul, the person lost to you could have been a ***whole*** soul and they **made their own arrangements with GOD**. They came to Earth without you, they had a certain path, purpose, and destiny, either with you if you two were correctly, spiritually matched, or without you, if you were not each other's destiny helpers, and **it was between that person and God as to when they would leave Earth.**

If you feel it was untimely, were you an intercessor, a prayer warrior for your person? Did you talk about the things of God, together, and both make godly choices in life, so the enemy had no footing against either of you? Had you both healed your ancestral foundations and bloodlines? Then what was happening even in your beloved's life was as much of a mystery to them as it was to you. No wonder you are shocked and surprised, maybe even traumatized.

If your departed person was *not* a whole soul and was living a tormented life, do you know for certain that there was spiritual protection around them and that *other* spiritual entities weren't working against their life? That's why I say it's blasphemy, how do you know what took that person's life? Do you know without a fact that didn't lay it down? Some people choose to go. So how can you categorically be angry with God?

There would be no way for you to have ANY clue if it was their time to go, except for old age, like if they were 150 years old. But still, no one is ever really "prepared" for the loss. How you feel in grief is human, it's normal. It's a process and you must continue the process of getting past it, or at least coping with the loss.

Like Jesus: weep, forgive and continue doing your purpose for being here on Earth with a right attitude, mindset, and spirit. Like God: set new order in your life.

The Upward Turn

God is the lifter of your head. Turn your head upward and thank God for what you had and for what you still have in your life. *""Lord if you never do another thing for me..."* people love to say that. Can you stand on that if you lose someone?

Instead of seeking after the comfort of your flesh, you need comfort in your soul and the Holy Spirit is the one who can do this for you. When you seek for comfort in your soul it is a sign that you are a child of God, you believe that God will, and He can. It is a sign that you have the Holy Spirit. It is a sign that you are maturing in God, you are not selfish, and that you care for others.

What are the signs that you are a child of God?

Do you like the attention from people while you are in this plight?

Do you feel it's your duty to grieve?

How is your life after compared to this time last year?

Accept the Comfort

Long-term grieving gets people a lot of attention…. When you get to the place of, This is enough about me you get out of a selfish mode, you've really grown. I don't mean if you just had a loss last week – but it's been a year, two years, or it's been a while….

When you start seeking after comfort for your **soul**, which is comprised of your mind, your will and your intellect, it is a sign that you care for yourself and others—that you ae not a *user*.

It is so difficult to be around someone unhappy, discontent, inconsolable. It can be frustrating when you're trying to comfort someone who won't be comforted. You may bring them gifts, you may love on them, sit with them--, but they just won't take your comfort…

Are you accepting the comfort of others?

Are you abusing the comfort/time/gifts/efforts of others?

Do you believe you are talking to your lost loved one?

The dead know nothing. They do not speak. The devil sends in demons in masks and masquerades to trick you. Saul thought he had summonsed Samuel from the dead; it was a demon, a *familiar spirit* (1 Samuel 28).

Talk to GOD, just talk to GOD.

God only. Repent of having done this. Renounce any covenants or contracts made by doing this and revoke every word you spoke to anyone that was not God, the Father, the Son or the Holy Spirit or an angel of the Only Living God, Jehovah.

When people seek after the comfort of their flesh, they don't want the comfort that the Word says they should have, they don't want the comfort that God prescribes, they want their own comfort. It's as though they are having a tantrum. *I want what I want to feel better, not what momma says, not what daddy says, not even what God says.* And most often that comfort will minister to the **flesh** not the soul. That comfort will be temporary, not lasting. You can minister to your flesh, but there is no JOY in that, no peace, and no enduring comfort.

This is a book of hard truths. I love you, but I didn't come to coddle you. I want you to stand up, rise up and celebrate what you had, the life you currently have, and the plans you can make to go forward.

Tidings of comfort and Joy was prophesied in the Old Testament. Jesus was born, then just 30 years from His birth, just one generation later, Jesus had released the Comforter into the Earth, a comfort the world had never known before

Exercise:

Do you believe your lost loved one is speaking to you?

> (Please know there is a *fantasy spirit spouse*.)

Is your perpetual grief getting you out of some things you don't want to do, like have another committed relationship?

Learn more about the Holy Spirit....

He said unto them, Have ye received the Holy Ghost since ye believed? And they said unto him, We have not so much as heard whether there be any Holy Ghost.

Acts 19:2

Some of what the Holy Spirit does for us:

The Holy Spirit is our Helper

The Holy Spirit is our **Comforter**

The Holy Spirit gives the Gifts of the Spirit:

- Discerning of spirits.

- Faith.

- Gifts of healings.

- Miracles.

- Prophecy.

Tongues and the interpretation of Tongues

- Word of knowledge

- Word of Wisdom

The Holy Spirit sanctifies us.

The Holy Spirit convicts us of sins.

The Holy Spirit brings things to our remembrance and leads us into all truth.

You've suffered a real loss. Go through the shock of it if it's recent. Now, we don't grieve like other folks grieve. We have a promise, we have an assurance that we will all meet up again and be together again and death has lost its sting.

Tidings of Comfort and Joy.

We do not want you to be uninformed, brothers and sisters, concerning **those** who are asleep, so that you will not **grieve** like the rest, **who have no hope.**

1 Thessalonians 4:13 CEB.

Exercise:

How is your grieving process different from the world's?

How is it the same as the world's way of grieving?

Is part of the problem that you don't understand death?

What things can you do better?

Joy Comes in the Morning

Is it morning yet?

Is the dark night of grief over? In the presence of the LORD is where you will find JOY, (Psalm 16:11). You've got to want it. You can't be like the baby that rejects the bottle.

Your joy is your faith that things are going to get better. Isn't that why you get out of bed anyway?

Joy is your receipt that things did get better.

The Lord has made me glad, (Psalm 92:4). I come rejoicing.

Things did get better because God said they would and now they have.

Your joy is the evidence that you've been in the presence of GOD and God wants your joy to be full.

How's my JOY on a scale from 1 to 10? Why?

What could make my life better? Realistically

Your Joy is proof that your spirit man is bigger than your natural man. When you are going *through* and it looks like you shouldn't be praising God, lifting holy hands, your Joy is proof that your spirit man is big enough to sustain you in times of trouble.

The natural man wants to get in the corner and curl up. Spirit man stands up and says, *"I WILL BLESS the Lord. I am going to enter into His gates with thanksgiving and into His courts with Praise. I will bless His name."* (Psalm 100:4)

He has made me precious promises, so I'm going to keep going.

The spirit of a man will sustain his infirmity;
but a wounded spirit who can bear?

(Proverbs 18:14)

*Who is bigger in your life right now, your spirit
man or your natural man(flesh)?*

*Joy proves that your true self is greater than
your flesh--*

Especially when you are going through.

Name some ways the Lord has made you glad:

*If JOY is speaking right now, what is she
saying to you?*

   Your Joy speaks of who you are and
that's when you're acting like your Heavenly
Father.

The Lord Himself has Joy--. IS Joy. There is not only rejoicing in His presence, but a fullness of Joy.

Grief and Depression are from the devil.

Your Joy is proof that your mind is good; it is proof that you have the mind of Christ. It is proof that you've got the Holy Spirit.

It is proof that you possess your soul.

Possess your soul so that your JOY can be full. Whomever, or whatever possesses your soul possesses your power and also possesses your JOY.

Your Joy is proof of who you are and who your DADDY (Abba) is.

Your Joy is proof that you are trusted. God said that if He can trust you with the little things, then you can be trusted with the big things.

Enter into the Joy of the Lord.

Let this mind be in you, which was also in
Christ Jesus: (Philippians 2:5)

Pray to receive the Mind of Christ:

*Where's my soul? Do I have full authority over
it or do things happen to me?*

*How's my soul? Is it well with my soul, right
now? (Mind, Will & Emotions)*

A lot of people have forgotten GOD and that they **can** have joy again. Your joy, either newfound or regained Joy is proof that your mind is good. Let this mind be in you that was also in Christ Jesus. *That* you remember and haven't forgotten is a sign that your mind is good, and you are in Christ, and He is in you.

Amen.

Exercise:

Is it fear? Is it that you are afraid of dying?

In case you missed this in the front of the book.

Prayer for Salvation in Jesus Christ

L ord, God I believe that Jesus is the Son of God the only begotten of the Father. I believe and confess that Jesus came to Earth and died on the Cross. On the third day, God resurrected Him. I believe in my heart and confess with my mouth that Jesus is Lord and I invite Him into my heart and my life today and I am saved.

Thank You, Father,

Amen.

Accepted salvation Date:

_____

Baptized: Date:

_____

Holy Spirit Filled Date:

_____

Depressed or going through? Down in the pits? In the Bible, David had to encourage *himself* in the Lord. You know why? Because he didn't have the Comforter. Jesus hadn't come yet. But you've got the Comforter...

Look in your Bible, take Bible study classes, listen to teaching or preaching messages, or some worship music, get into the presence of God to get your joy back. Pray the Lord restores your soul.

Saul got in the dumps, a lot. It was so bad that he wanted to KILL the person that was trying to drive the evil spirit out of him. David was there to cheer Saul, but Saul (Saul's demons) wanted to kill David. Talk about not taking another person's comfort...

Some cranky folks treat their caregivers so badly. They need Jesus, and deliverance. They need to be saved and they need Comfort. They need the presence of God. It is healing, uplifting, joy-giving.

Tidings of Comfort and Joy to you.

Jesus also came to heal and comfort people – others wanted kill him.

Saul was so overcome because he was so deep into sin and witchcraft. There was no Godly protection for Saul anymore. Saul wanted evil more than he wanted God. What's in you wields a lot of power. You have to get the sin out of your life to receive God's comfort. You can't have sin and comfort because I remind you that sin has torment. Saul was tormented, for sure.

Anniversaries of negative events and memories of people you've lost can be very painful, but don't let the devil use it as a hook to pull you down into the spiral of darkness and night again.

Grieve if you have to, grieve if you are called to – for a season, but go into the next season, the next year with your soul prospering…not limping weak and wounded. You don't need to put on a performance for anyone to "prove" your relationship with that lost person was *"all that."*

You don't have to overact or keep it all together; be yourself. Fall apart if you have to but fall into the arms of Jesus and then fall back together as soon as you can.

You are a whole person able to stand and move and have *being*, even without the person or people that you've loved so much and that have also loved you so much. You make them proud.

When you get to Glory, *you* will have to report on your exploits that defined and improved your *family line*. *That* grandma, mom, dad or another loved one is gone means you have to **grow up** some more and work harder, not-- quit. You now have the baton to make your family bloodline look good when God looks on you and all the people who have your DNA.

Else, what was the purpose in all that they taught you and imparted to you?

Do A New Thing

Not having comfort and joy is not prospering to your soul.

Behold I do a new thing (Isaiah 43:19). Why not surprise your flesh this time? This year, this season do a new thing. Let your spirit man surprise your flesh. Tell it to do something new. You've got the Spirit of God in you, so do a new thing. Surprise your flesh and tell it what it's going to do this time instead of letting your flesh run the show. Your flesh will tell you to go to the liquor store, buy this, drink that, look for this sort of entertainment.

If it's not of God don't do it.

Invitations go out all the time – especially from the devil: Pity party over here, over there… everywhere. You're the guest of honor, you are the center of attention. This time, this year, this season, do something new – don't accept the invite. Break that programmed **cycle of grief** off your life. Don't GO to the pity party. Refuse the pity party, it's a form of **idolatry**, where you're the star. You get to go over and over in your mind or to whomever will listen to you how bad it is for you, what *they* did to you, what you don't have, what you want, what you wish you had, how discontented and sad you are. How much of a wilderness person you are.

But you don't see that wilderness part – that's why you have the Holy Spirit to bring you under conviction. You have the Holy Spirit, the Word of GOD which is powerful, sharper than a two-edged sword. This is where you need the mind of Christ. So, you know how to use it.

Comfort is not pity. Comfort is compassion, but it is not extended pity, perpetual grief, or being babied. Comfort is somebody of God saying what God says about you, to you, reminding you of who you are, putting a picture of yourself in your face to remind you that you are *called*, chosen, blessed, set apart and that you don't grieve like unsaved people. And reminding you that you're not a wilderness person going around the same mountain, a Mountain of Grief, for 40 years, 80 years, all your life.

Reminding you that you are going somewhere; you're not at a standstill. Right?

Exercise:

What is the pattern of my or my family's grief?

Nothing Is the Same

The longer you grieve the longer you hang on to a hurt, grief or trauma, is a sign of how soul tied you are to a person or thing. Yeah, people can be soul-tied to *things*. The more soul tied, and the less willing you are to let go of it.

Hoarders are in grief; and Grief is in them. It's hard to separate a hoarder from *things and stuff* because **they want things to remain the same.** But in grief, nothing is the same.

Pray this Prayer:

Lord, the Word says Blessed are they that mourn for they shall be comforted. Comfort me, Lord as I go through this loss, this disappointment, in the Name of Jesus. Father, draw a line between healthy grief, healthy, necessary grieving and the *spirit of grief* or *heaviness*. I bind up the *spirit of grief* and I send it back to the pit of hell where it came from. I reject it. I renounce ever entertaining it and Lord rebuke it in the name of Jesus. Father all other *spirits* that have entered my life with prolonged grief, scatter them with the wind of God, never to return to me again, in the Name of Jesus. Amen.

As a matter of fact, your goal, in grief was probably to **make** things stay the same because you didn't want anything else to change. It's a desire for control. But everything has changed. I could say except you, but that's not true. You're worse.

Grief is a trap. Grief is the thing that people accept that is trying to lead them to where the person they are grieving is: <u>Gone</u>. I'm not saying heaven or hell for them; I don't know where they are, but hopefully it's heaven.

The *spirit of grief* comes to woo you to death. If not quickly, then slowly will do. Grief is trying to kill you. That is the purpose of it. Don't agree with it. Don't expect it. Don't accept it. Don't let it sit down in your house or get comfortable your life. Don't talk with it, except to tell it to GET OUT! When you are "talking to your dearly departed" THEY AREN'T THERE. You are talking to a demon.

I'm sorry to say that your beloved is not in the graveyard. Dressing a headstone or grave is considered respectable in our culture, but you lost loved one is not there; the dead know nothing, they are gone, (Ecclesiastes 9:5).

Turning a headstone into an altar, by talking to it--, talking to a piece of granite or decorative cement, every day, or very often, taking flowers, tears, and words to that spot is all worship. We'd all like to think that heavenly angels are there watching over the last place we may have seen our loved one(s).

I haven't found that in the Bible.

If you're soul-tied, part of your soul may be in the graveyard with the person that you've tied yourself to. Bob jogs every day. He jogs to the graveyard where his deceased wife is buried and will never move from the house they lived in together since it's close to the graveyard. He's very angry and doesn't even realize it. Five years have passed; he wants to date, but he's cruel to women he meets because of his anger.

Grief, chronic grief, heaviness, pining away, depression, anger, means you've been *captured*. As such no matter how much, you cry or blame God, you can do NOTHING for the person you are grieving over. Our spiritual power is in the wholeness of our soul. We need to possess a whole soul.

While you were locked in your room, or on your crying couch, while you weren't looking, or possibly self-medicated, the devil has changed the whole game; it's another whole arena, it's another whole game – it's another whole sport and you didn't even think that anything had changed.

You should be fighting, spiritually, but your fight is not with God. Plus, why would anyone try to fight **God**, anyway? Know your adversary. The devil is the one who has changed the game. As far as the devil is concerned, transactions with your lost loved one are over; **you are the target now**. You desperately need to be defending yourself, your family, things, stuff and your very life. Grief has caused you to wander into the enemy's camp and be captured.

No amount of yearning can make it the way it was again; you can't make time stand still and have nothing change ever again. It must; everything living *changes*.

If you fight to keep your own soul, you can pray, TO GOD for your loved one's life and eternal comfort. Let them rest in peace.

It must; everything living *changes*. It must, and it will.

Deliverance is Love

Do you know what can happen at a funeral, at a graveyard? It's best to be prayed up if you go to one.

The Headstone becomes the altar; the grief is the worship. The attention is the worship –pouring libations on the ground are drink offerings to the devil or other evil entity is not cool, it's demonic.

Ancestral worship--, see that you do it not. Making a favorite meal, leaving an empty seat for that person, is not of God, and it is not honoring the deceased.

Cremains still in the house; let the dead bury their dead, (Luke 9:60).

The unusual customs and acts that people do in grief that are not in the Bible, that are not of God--, I think most people think they are honoring their lost loved one(s). They think this is love. It is NOT love.

LOVE is Deliverance. If you're not getting *delivered* from something you say or do**, but instead getting deeper in bondage; that is NOT LOVE.**

Turn your head to the sky, turn it upward and look past the hills from whence cometh your help and thank God for your past, present and future. Thank God for your destiny and your bloodline. Thank God for your future and your good successes. Press forward; give God a sacrifice of praise and seek to enter into His presence where there are pleasures at His Right Hand, forevermore. Amen.

YOU have to do something on your own because YOU desire to move forward out of the miry clay, out of darkness, out of the pit, out of the dark waters If you do, if you pray and ask, God will set you in a large place, a prosperous place.

Deliverance from Grief

Father, in the Name of Jesus, I RENOUNCE the devious *spirit of grief.* Yes, blessed are those that mourn because You have compassion on them and you comfort and heal them, binding up broken hearts, in the Name of Jesus. Lord, I ask for complete deliverance from Grief today while still respecting the loss that I've endured.

Thank You Lord for the times where I did have _____ . I bless You now, and I bless them. Thank You for the life I'm still living, may I bring honor and glory to Your name as I continue forward in life. Light my path so I'll go in the right direction. Holy Spirit be with me, urge me when I need it Angels of God, be my protection in the Name of Jesus.

Thank You, Lord, for bringing me past the stages of grief, I'm no longer in denial. *Spirit of anger*, I bind you, the Lord Jesus rebuke you. I will not sin in anger in the Name of Jesus. I will make no devil deals or ask for anything ungodly or unholy in this process.

Depression, you are bound and cast out, forever, in the Name of Jesus. Lord, Let me accept the loss, this transition in my life, but not the *spirit of grief, heaviness*, evil load, bitterness, hatred, anger or unforgiveness in the Name of Jesus.

I am pressing forward, I'm going somewhere, Lord. Please bring me through this Wilderness of Grief.

Heal me, Lord. Make me whole again, emotionally and mentally whole. Physically whole. Lord, restore my soul, Light of the World shine on me and erase the blues out of my life, in the Name of Jesus.

Amen.

Christian books by this author

AK: Adventures of the Agape Kid

AMONG SOME THIEVES

As My Soul Prospers

Behave

Churchzilla (The Wanna-Be Bride of Christ)

The Coco-So-So Correct Show

Demons Hate Questions

Devil Weapons: *Anger, Unforgiveness & Bitterness*

Do Not Orphan Your Seed

Do Not Work for Money

Don't Refuse Me Lord

The FAT Demons

got Money?

Let Me Have a Dollar's Worth

Living for the NOW of God

Lord, Help My Debt

Lose My Location

Made Perfect In Love

The Man Safari *(Really, I'm Just Looking)*

Marriage Ed., *Rules of Engagement & Marriage*

The Motherboard: *Key to Soul Prosperity*

Name Your Seed

Plantation Souls

The Poor Attitudes of Money

Power Money: Nine Times the Tithe

The Power of Wealth

Seasons of Grief

Seasons of War

SOULS in Captivity

Soul Prosperity: Your Health & Your Wealth

The *spirit* **of Poverty**

The Throne of Grace, *Courtroom Prayers*

Time Is of the Essence

Triangular Powers (4 book series)

Warfare Prayer Against Poverty

When the Devourer is Rebuked

The Wilderness Romance

<u>Other Journals & Devotionals by this author:</u>

The Cool of the Day – Journal

got HEALING? Verses for Life

got HOPE? Verses for Life

got WISDOM? Verses for Life

got GRACE? Verses for Life

got JOY? Verses for Life

got PEACE? Verses for Life

got LOVE? Verses for Life

He Hears Us, Prayer Journal *4 colors*

I Have A Star, Dream Journal *kids, teen,   young adult and up.*

I Have A Star, Guided Prayer Journal,

J'ai une Etoile, Journal des Reves

Let Her Dream, Dream Journal

Men Shall Dream, Dream Journal,

My Favorite Prayers (in 4 styles)

My Sowing Journal (in three different colors)

Tengo una Estrella, Diario de Sueños

<u>Illustrated children's books by this author:</u>

Big Dog (8-book series)

Do Not Say That to Me

Every Apple

Fluff the Clouds

I Love You All Over the World

Imma Dance

The Jump Rope

Kiss the Sun

The Masked Man

Not During a Pandemic

Push the Wind

Tangled Taffy

What If?

Wiggle, Wiggle; Giggle, Giggle

Worry About Yourself

You Did Not Say Goodbye to Me

Thank you for purchasing this volume, we pray for your complete healing and deliverance, in the Name of Jesus.

Amen.

About the Author

Dr. Marlene Miles has served in ministry for 20+ years. She holds two Doctorate degrees in Ministry and is a dentist.

Enjoy Bible teaching and messages on the Dr. Miles YouTube Channel.

Find spiritual warfare prayers on the Warfare Prayer Channel on YouTube.